A STREET
THROUGH TIME

ILLUSTRATION: STEVE NOON

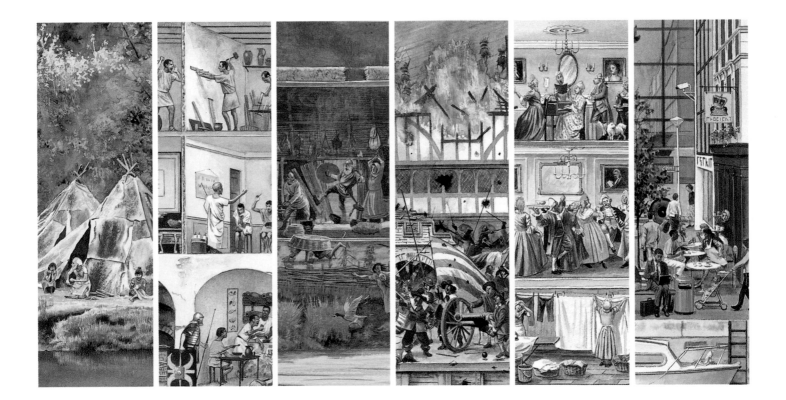

London, New York,
Melbourne, Munich, and Delhi

Senior Art Editor Sheila Collins
Editor Matilda Gollon
Managing Editor Linda Esposito
Managing Art Editor Diane Peyton Jones
Category Publisher Laura Buller
Publishing Director Jonathan Metcalf
Associate Publishing Director Liz Wheeler
Art Director Phil Ormerod
Production Editor Adam Stoneham
Senior Production Controller Sophie Argyris
Jacket Designer Laura Brim
Jacket Editor Manisha Majithia

DK India
Art Editors Neha Sharma, Shipra Jain
Senior Art Editor Sudakshina Basu
Managing Art Editor Arunesh Talapatra
DTP Designer Anita Yadav
DTP Manager Balwant Singh

First published in the United States in 2012 by
DK Publishing
345 Hudson Street
New York, New York 10014

24 26 28 29 27 25 23
023–185833– 09/12

A catalog record for this book is available
from the Library of Congress.

ISBN: 978-0-7566-9792-1

Hi-res workflow proofed by MDP, UK
Printed and bound in China

Discover more at
www.dk.com

CONTENTS

THE STORY OF A STREET

Some streets and even some whole towns are very new, but there are some towns and streets that are very old. Come with us and explore an old, old street. You will see how it has changed from a camp of nomadic hunter-gatherers, into a settled village, then a town, and then a city. Its progress has by no means been smooth! Sometimes the people living there have enjoyed peace and prosperity. At other times they have faced war, sickness, and poverty. Some buildings in the street have survived, while others have been rebuilt many, many times. You'll also find out how people's way of life and standard of living have changed—not always for the better!

A RIVERSIDE SETTLEMENT

The river is central to the story of our street. Around 12,000 years ago, it drew Stone Age hunters, pleased to have a good water supply and a handy source of fish! About 4,000 years ago, when farming had replaced hunting as a way of life, the river provided water for people, animals, and crops, as well as fish to eat. Later the river brought trade to the village, helping it grow and prosper. But the river sometimes brought troubles, too, such as invaders and disease. You can trace the changing role of the river from age to age as the story of the street unfolds.

CHANGING TIMES

For hundreds of years people farmed and lived in the village by the river. The farmers' lives changed only slowly until the arrival of the Romans caused a total upheaval! By about 100 CE the village had become a town with all the benefits of Rome's comfortable way of life. The local people lived in small apartments and traditional huts, while the Romans occupied villas and large houses. Everything changed again when Rome's empire was invaded by barbarians. The town was destroyed, our street became part of a small village, and people's standard of living plummeted. The struggle to survive and prosper began anew. But it was to be shattered again, this time by Vikings in 900 CE.

THE TIME TRAVELER

This is Henry Hyde. He is hidden in the picture of each historical period. Henry works in a museum, but he has a secret: He has a time-machine. He can travel back to the past and see how people lived and how the objects, now in his museum, were used. See how many times you can spot him!

FROM VILLAGE TO CITY

Eventually, powerful kings and lords put an end to the Viking threat. Traders who now sailed up the river helped the village grow into a town. By the late 1600s the town had survived plagues and wars, though the castle was reduced to ruins. The real changes came in the late 1700s and early 1800s. Improvements in farming methods meant more people could be fed by fewer farmers on less land. Inventions brought the Industrial Revolution to our street, which was now in a rapidly growing city. There were new industries, new methods of transportation, and new wealth. However, for some, life became even harder.

THE STREET TODAY

Our street remains in a city that has survived wars and spread so far that all the old forests and farmland have disappeared. The pace of change has become so rapid that people who lived in our street only 150 years ago would not recognize the modern businesses along the riverbank. People are much better off now than their ancestors. But what will happen over the next 100 years?

STONE AGE (10,000 BCE)

Once upon a time, everyone lived by hunting, fishing, and gathering food. People were nomads, moving across the land in small groups seeking food and shelter. This tribe has just found a good spot to spend the winter. The river will provide a fresh water supply and lots of fish to eat! The camp is the start of our street.

Deer skull (symbol of the woodland god)

Preparing animal hide

Priest

Gathering berries

Storyteller

Chopping wood

Fishing

NO WASTE
The animals' meat is eaten, their fur and hides make clothes and tents, and their bones make tools.

STOCKED UP
Some of the meat is dried and stored, ready for the winter months.

FOREST SPIRIT
The tribe's priest is calling on the spirit of the forest to bless the new camp.

CRAFTY CANOE
The canoes are made from tree trunks, gathered from the surrounding forest.

IN THE STICKS
Forest stretches across the land and there are very few people. The camp is isolated.

MAN'S BEST FRIEND
Dogs are the only animals that people have tamed. Find the dogs fighting over food scraps.

Animal hide tent

Cutting Meat

Flint worker

Hunters

Making a fire

Plucking a duck

Making a canoe

FINDING FLINT
Tools and weapons are made of flint. This flint worker has found a good source nearby.

FRUIT PICKING
The women use digging sticks to help them gather berries, nuts, and roots.

A GOOD CATCH
Fish are caught with nets made from plant fibers. They are weighed down with stones.

FIRST FARMERS (2,000 BCE)

More than eight thousand years have passed and people have learned how to grow crops and keep animals. They have also developed new skills, such as pottery making, weaving cloth, and metalworking. The site by the river now has a permanent settlement of wooden huts with thatched roofs made from straw.

Stone circle

Using a bow and arrow

Thatched wooden hut

Palisade

Weaving

Hunter

Spinning

Pottery kiln

Sewing

Threshing

Winnowing

Harpooning fish

SACRED STONES

Several villages have joined together to build a stone circle to honor the gods.

NEW CLOTHES

Clothes are now made from woolen cloth as well as leather and fur. The women spin, weave, and sew.

CLAY POTS

This man is using river clay to make pots for the settlement.

LIVESTOCK
The people have started to keep cattle, pigs, sheep, and goats for meat and milk.

GOOD SHOT
The people have invented a useful weapon for hunting: the bow and arrow.

UP IN SMOKE
Fire is a great danger in wooden huts with thatched roofs. It can spread quickly.

Barrow

Cutting crops

Cutting firewood

Blacksmith

Roasting meat

Grinding wheat

Making a basket

Metal mold

Making flint tools

KEEP OUT!
A wooden palisade around the village protects the people from wild animals.

GROWING GRAINS
Wheat and barley grow in the fields. The crops are cut with a sickle made from a sharp piece of flint.

BARROW
Members of one family are buried in a grave covered by a mound of earth.

IRON AGE (600 BCE)

Many hundreds of years pass. People have found out how to produce the metal iron and they use it to make better tools and weapons. The village has prospered, but there are battles with neighboring tribes, who are fierce rivals. The chief has built a fort on the hillside to protect the village from invasion.

Ancient stone circle

Sacred grove

Enemy heads

Guard

Thatched wooden hut

Cattle

Rival warriors

Palisade

Loom

Tattooing

Pottery kiln

Fishing

Foreign trader

Wooden boat

TOP MAN
After the warriors and the priests, the blacksmith is the most important man in the village.

STEALING CATTLE
A rival tribe has arrived to steal the villagers' cattle. They have traveled here on a wheeled wagon.

RIVER RITUAL
Priests offer captured enemy weapons to the gods by throwing them into the river.

BOATING
Little boats called coracles are made out of sticks and animal skin.

FANCY OUTFITS
The people have used natural dyes found in earth and plants to make colorful cloths.

WOODEN FORT
The chief has built a stronghold, called a fort, on the hill. It is made of wood.

Fort

Ancient barrow

Chief

Thatchers

Plowing

Carpenter

Prisoners

Blacksmith

Priests

Coracle

FAST FARMING
To help people farm, a more efficient plow has been invented. It is made from iron.

EXOTIC GOODS
A foreign trader has sailed up the river. The villagers are eager to buy his wine, silverware, and pots.

WOODEN STATUES
Can you find three wooden statues set up by the villagers to honor the gods?

ROMAN TIMES (100 CE)

The Roman Empire has spread across much of Europe, bringing a new way of life. Our village has become a town with hundreds of people. The town has large stone and brick buildings, shops, taverns, a temple, and a school. A bridge has been built across the river for the first time. Professional soldiers are stationed in the fort.

Statue of the Roman god Jupiter

Temple

Ancient stone circle

Apartment

Carpenters

Wall paintings

School

Pottery shop

Tavern

Baker's shop

Slaves

Local hunter

Domus

Bedroom

Bedroom

Bathroom

Kitchen

Atrium

Stove

Wooden bridge

SLAVE LABOR

Most hard work is done by slaves. Find a batch of slaves arriving in their chains.

NATIVE HUTS

Some of the inhabitants of the old village still live in their wooden, thatched huts.

EATING OUT

Most people go to the taverns for hot food because they live in small apartments that do not have kitchens.

SCHOOL DAYS
Children from rich families attend school. Can you find the schoolroom where a lesson is taking place?

TOWN HOUSE
A rich family lives in a town house, called a domus. The domus has beautiful statues and paintings.

BATHTIME
People use the luxurious bathhouse in the town to bathe or just to relax and socialize.

Native huts

Fort

Roman soldiers

Amphitheater

Wine warehouse

Basilica (law cases held here)

Bathhouse

Crane

Brick building

Fountain

Merchant ship

Imported wine in amphorae

IMPORTED GOODS
Merchant ships bring goods from all over the Empire. Wine is stored in containers called amphorae.

READY FOR ACTION
The fort is where Roman soldiers are stationed. They drill and march, so they are always ready for action.

CROWD-PLEASER
In the amphitheater, gladiators often fight to the death to amuse the crowd.

17

THE INVADERS (600 CE)

Barbarian tribes have swept across Europe, destroying the Roman way of life. A group have settled in the ruins of our town. All the Roman comforts, such as baths and piped water, have been forgotten. People are living in wooden huts again, growing vegetables, and hunting in the surrounding forests.

Sheep pen

Wolves

Columns from Roman temple

Shepherd boy

Thatched wooden hut

Chief

Weaving

Laying fish traps

Wooden boat

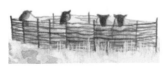

FENCED IN
Sticks are used to make wooden fences. This keeps the sheep from straying.

PRECIOUS TIMBER
Wood is used for cooking, heating, and building. Find five people chopping or gathering wood.

MYSTERY SHIELD
This woman has found a strange shield in the river. Do you remember when it was used?

OUT OF ORDER
The Roman bathrooms have been destroyed so there is very little privacy.

MODEST DWELLINGS
The simple huts are made of wood. The chief has the biggest hut and he has displayed a hunting trophy over the door.

BIG BAD WOLF
Wolves have taken a sheep. The shepherd boy tries to drive them away with his sling.

Roman fort

Ancient barrow

Roman amphitheater

Chief's hut

Dried meat

Beggars

Blacksmith

Carpenter

Vegetable patch

Washing clothes

Coracle

TROTTING AROUND
Pigs roam through the village, scavenging. This one takes a bite out of the laundry!

FRESH FISH
The fish traps will help provide the villagers with extra fresh food.

ON THE HUNT
The chief and his son have been out hunting. The wild boar they have killed will be a welcome addition to the food stores.

VIKING RAIDERS (900 CE)

The barbarians have now been settled for hundreds of years. They have become Christians and have grown prosperous. They have a king who gives his orders through the local chiefs. Now a new danger has appeared—fierce Viking raiders have arrived from Scandinavia and are seeking booty and slaves.

Ancient stone circle

Hole for fire smoke

Stone church

Graveyard

Toilet

Viking longship

Viking

SELF DEFENSE
An iron cooking pot can be a good weapon! This family may just be able to escape.

PRECIOUS BOOTY
The church has gold and silver ornaments that attract raiders, but its books are likely to be burned.

HIDING PLACES
Find a person hiding in a barrel, another under a table, and another under a basket.

SOLD AS SLAVES
The people flee. Women and children will be sold into slavery if they are captured by the raiders.

PRAYING PRIEST
The priest hopes that his prayers will drive back the raiders and leave the town in peace. Can you find him?

STONE CHURCH
Unlike the huts, the church is built of stone and will not burn down easily.

Ancient barrow

Chief's hall with wooden roof

Thatched wooden hut

Jetty

DAWN RAID
Two boatloads of Vikings have rowed quietly up the river before dawn and taken the villagers by surprise.

OCCUPIED
The village has an outdoor toilet. A very awkward place to be caught during a raid!

BURIED TREASURE
The villagers are in a panic. Some try to hide their valuables by burying them underground.

MEDIEVAL VILLAGE (1200s)

More than three hundred years have passed. The king has given land to a lord, who has built a castle to control the area. The Lord rents the land to mounted warriors, called knights for their support in defending the village. Peasants have been granted small strips of land from the knights in return for work in the fields, or payments of money or goods.

Ancient stone circle

Common land

Spire

Fallow land (unplanted)

Glass windows (used by the church and rich only)

Church

Peasant's house

Cobbler's shop

Baker's shop

Reed cutter's boat

UPRIVER
It's cheaper to bring goods by river and safer, too—there may be outlaws in the forest!

MARKET MINSTRELS
Find the entertainers in the marketplace playing music for the crowds. They are called minstrels.

COMMON GROUND
Villagers use the common to graze livestock such as sheep and cattle. Can you find this land?

EXOTIC CLOTH

The lord's wife is buying cloth from a foreign merchant. Can you find them?

MARKET DAY

Today is market day. Some people have come from other villages to buy and sell goods.

STRIPS OF LAND

The village has three fields. Each villager has strips of land in each field.

Keep

Stone castle

Windmill on site of ancient barrow

Miller's house

Castle wall

Barley strips growing

Wheat strips growing

Chimney

Timber-framed house

Knight's stone house

Dentist

Inn

Milkmaid

Blacksmith

Peddler

Foreign merchant

Sailboat

STONE CASTLE

The lord has built a stone castle. From it, he can control all the surrounding land.

FOUL PLAY

A ball game with boys from the neighboring village is turning into a rowdy riot!

FLOUR POWER

Villagers grind their grain in the lord's mill. They think the miller keeps some of their flour!

MEDIEVAL TOWN (1400s)

Thanks to the trade brought by boats up the river, the village has now grown into a town. Its citizens have purchased a charter from their lord. This gives them more rights and allows them to run the town. Some of the merchants have become very rich, and can afford to improve their houses and shops.

Collecting firewood

Church

Wine merchant's house

Bedroom

Doctor

Shutter

Barber's shop

Kitchen

Cobbler's shop

Weaver's shop

Religious procession

Merchant lending money

Selling wine

Cellar

Stone bridge

CONVENIENCES
Rich citizens can afford to have expensive glass in their windows and an indoor toilet—of a sort!

SKILLED WORK
Craftsmen have formed guilds. These unions protect the craftsmen and set standards of work.

CLEAN WATER?
Most people still have to get their drinking water from the dirty river.

INN TROUBLE
Can you guess what the rowdy inn is called from the sign hanging outside it?

WATCH OUT!
Household waste gets thrown out into the street. Can you see who is in for a nasty shock?

PAST RELICS
A man has found an ancient helmet in the river—who do you think once wore it?

Turret

Stone castle

Miller's house

Windmill

Town guard

Deer hunters

Gibbet

Guildhall

Tapestry

Glass window

Market cross

Inn

Stocks

Armorer's workshop

Black rats come off ship

Foreign merchant's ship

Lord and his wife return from a trip

REMODELING
The lord is making improvements to his castle to make it more comfortable.

A GRISLY END
Petty thieves are placed in the stocks, and the gibbet is used to hang murderers.

OPEN SHOP
In the bustling town, shop fronts are lowered and used as counters by the shopkeepers.

THE PLAGUE STRIKES! (1500s)

The Black Death arrived in Europe from the Far East in 1347, carried by the fleas on black rats. Over the next three hundred years it kept returning. Most people who caught the plague died. This disease has now hit our prosperous town, and the people are trying to stop everyone from catching it.

Plague pit

Church

Merchant's house

Painting a white cross

Baker's shop

Death cart

Kitchen

Burglars

Printing press

Cellar

Soldiers

 MARK OF DEATH
A white cross on a door shows there is plague inside. No one can leave the house.

 SMELLY SULFUR
Sulfur is burned in the street to try to get rid of the deadly infection. It has a nasty smell!

 **BREAKING IN**
Thieves are taking advantage of a family's illness by stealing their valuables.

USING FORCE
To prevent the plague from spreading, soldiers have been sent to stop people from leaving town.

FINDING A CURE
Find the apothecary mixing a potion in his shop to find a cure for the plague.

BRAVE PRIEST
Although the priest is frightened of catching the plague, he still tends to a dying man.

Windmill

Miller's house

Stone castle

Gibbet

Guildhall

Inn

Doctor

Apothecary's shop

PLAGUE PITS
A cart collects the dead and takes them to a plague pit where the bodies are buried together.

SPOTTING SYMPTOMS
Black spots under the arms were a sign of plague. Which poor person has just found these symptoms?

INFESTATION
The open sewers in the streets attract the rats. They are everywhere now!

UNDER ATTACK! (1600s)

Disputes over territory and new ideas about religion have boiled over into violence, and the town is under attack. Enemy soldiers have invaded the town, setting fire to buildings and stealing valuables. The enemy is armed with deadly new weapons, and not even the strong castle walls can withstand the pounding of the powerful new cannons.

Enemy soldiers

Church

Cobblers shop

Weavers shop

Kitchen

Merchant's house

Printing press

Town soldiers

ENEMY TROOPS
Enemy soldiers surround the town and many have broken in, killing, destroying, and stealing.

NEW WEAPONS
Cannons have been around a long time, but the new designs are much more powerful.

ROOFTOP RESCUE
Some people climb onto the roof of their house, hoping they can escape from the enemy.

LOOK OUT!
A soldier has been hit by a falling shop sign while trying to flee from the enemy. Can you spot him?

SHH!
Two people are trying to keep out of trouble by hiding under the bed. Can you find them?

POINTY PIKE
Can you find the innkeeper being threatened with a pike, a nasty weapon carried by footsoldiers?

Stone castle

Windmill

Miller's house

Doctor

Stone house

Inn

Cannon

OUCH!
Painkillers do not exist yet, but the doctor has to cut off a patient's shattered leg anyway.

GREAT ESCAPE
People are in a panic. Some try to hide their valuables, while others try to escape with them.

LOADED MUSKETS
The soldiers use guns called muskets. They fire only one bullet, then have to be reloaded.

AN AGE OF ELEGANCE (1700s)

Peace has returned and the town is prospering again. Some houses have been repaired, while others have been rebuilt in the latest style. The wealthy citizens have a lot of spare time. They pride themselves on their polite manners, their learning, and their elegant parties. Their servants still live in small living quarters.

Spire

Church

Clock

Servants' bedroom

Servants' bedroom

Brick building

Wife's bedroom

Husband's bedroom

Bedroom

Reading room

Reading poetry

Playing cards

Shoe shop

Dress shop

Wig shop

Dancing

Living room

Laundry room

Kitchen

Milkmaid

STATELY HOME
The new lord has left the ruined castle and now lives in a beautiful mansion.

NEW DECOR
Plaster and colorful wallpaper have replaced the old wooden paneling inside the houses.

HIGHWAYMAN
An outlaw has arrived in town and has broken into someone's house, looking for valuables to steal.

TRENDY WIGS
Wigs are very fashionable now. This man is choosing a new one from a selection in the wig shop.

STREET SELLERS
Some people make a living by selling fruit, flowers, and other goods in the busy street.

SWEEPING SOOT
Can you find the chimney sweep and his climbing boy on their way to work?

Squire's house

Castle ruins

Lord's mansion

Town hall

Inn

Guest room

Highwayman

Guest room

Statue

Stagecoach

Bar

Mail coach

Sedan chair

Rat-catcher

Coffeehouse

Chimney sweep

Hat shop

Sailboat

COFFEEHOUSE
Recently, coffee has been imported and has become a fashionable drink.

FAST COACH
A mail coach speeds out of the inn. These coaches carry passengers as well as mail from town to town.

TRAVEL IN STYLE
Sedan chairs are used by wealthy people so that they can travel in comfort through the streets.

GRIM TIMES (EARLY 1800s)

Coal has been discovered nearby. New industries with machines powered by steam have moved into the town, and factories have been built to house them. People from the countryside have come to work in these factories. The factory owners make a lot of money but their workers have to live and work in terrible conditions.

Holes in the roof are covered up

Church

Factory chimneys

Servant's room

Waste being emptied

Families share tiny rooms

Bathtub

Rooms for poor families

Living room

Shoe shop

Baker's shop

Bathroom

Dress shop

Ironmonger's shop

Factory owner's office

Kitchen

AIR POLLUTION
The air is now polluted by the smoke bellowing from all the factory chimneys.

UP, UP, AND AWAY!
A few brave men are experimenting with a new form of travel. Can you find them?

ON THE STREETS
There are no homes to look after orphans. Some live and sleep on the street.

CHILD WORKERS
Poor children have to work too, so that they can earn money. Most cannot read or write.

RIVER BARGE
Heavy goods such as coal are carried by barges. The barges are pulled along by horses on the riverbank.

DRIP DROP
Find the man whose roof is leaking. He can't afford to repair it.

Hot-air balloon

Factory

Castle ruins

Coal mines

Pottery kiln

Mansion

Town hall

Gambling

Pickpockets

Inn

Pawnbroker's shop

Liquor shop

Milk cart

Orphans

Coal barge

WATCH OUT!
These nasty men are using children to pick pockets in the street for them.

DANGEROUS DRINKING
Some people drink to forget their misery. This drunk has had a little too much and is in danger of falling off the roof!

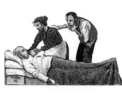

TAKEN ILL
With the overcrowding, dirt, and polluted water many people become ill.

FROM TOWN TO CITY (LATE 1800s)

Thanks to its industries, the town has grown into a city. Many people are better off, and working and living conditions have improved. A new railroad line now begins in our street and carries people and goods to other towns or cities. Steamboats chug along the river and people can hop on and off the horse-drawn omnibuses that travel around the city.

Church

Nursery

Bedroom

Bedroom

Bathroom

Lacing a corset

Master study

Living room

Draper's shop

Stockroom

Kitchen

Train station

Station restaurant

Steam engine

Ticket office

Mailbox

Lamplighter

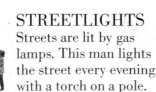

STREETLIGHTS
Streets are lit by gas lamps. This man lights the street every evening with a torch on a pole.

STEAMBOAT
Steam engines are now used to power riverboats as well as locomotives.

ON THE BEAT
Policemen now patrol the streets to keep order and fight crime.

CHOO-CHOO!
For the first time, people can travel long distances quickly and cheaply using the new railroads.

IN THE MAIL
A cheap postal service has been set up. Where do people mail their letters?

SMILE!
The photographer is about to take a picture of the men who are going to try out their new diving suits.

Factory chimneys

Growing suburbs

Castle ruins

Inventor

Guest rooms

City hall

Restaurant

Omnibus

Public bar

Saloon bar

Toy shop

Shoe shop

Inn

Road sweeper

Cellar

Steam pleasure boat

Photographer

CITY BUS
People can travel around the city cheaply using the horse-drawn omnibus. How many can you see?

PEDAL POWER
Although it was not very common, some daring women rode bicycles.

TOWN HOUSES
People who have made fortunes from factories have built houses away from the city center.

THE STREET TODAY

Our city has changed a lot since the 19th century. Modern businesses have replaced most heavy industries, people have become more environmentally aware, and leisure time has increased for many people. Landmarks from the different eras remain, but many have become tourist attractions, bringing visitors to the city.

Office building

Crane

Apartments

Hairdresser's salon

Artist's studio

Church

Dentist

Bathroom

Lawyer's office

Café

Museum

Bookstore

Gift shop

Clothing store

Bank

Gym

Vault

Jogger

Rowboat

SUNKEN TREASURE

Men dredging the river have found a chest on the riverbed. Who dropped it there and when?

FLYING OFF

Large passenger planes enable people to travel abroad easily and quickly.

GOING GREEN

The city is starting to use renewable energy from this wind farm.

CITY HERITAGE
The castle is now a protected historical monument and an important tourist attraction for the city.

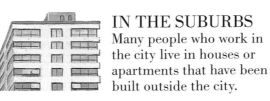

IN THE SUBURBS
Many people who work in the city live in houses or apartments that have been built outside the city.

NEW TECHNOLOGY
People rely on new technology for work and leisure, such as computers and cell phones.

Castle ruins

Tourists

Nursery

Bathroom

City hall

Living room

Kitchen

Café

Shoe store

Streetcar

Wine bar

Antique store

Restaurant

Motor cruiser

Dredger

Canoe

MODERN ARCHITECTURE
There is a handsome new city hall. Look how much glass has been used to build it! Modern streetcars pass by, carrying commuters and tourists.

CITY MUSEUM
Trains no longer use the railroad station. It is now a museum, housing objects from the past.

DOING CHORES
Inventions such as washing machines and vacuum cleaners make domestic work easier for everyone.

TIMELINE

As our street evolved, so did the rest of the world around it. Retrace the 12,000-year journey to find out what was happening just around the corner or on the other side of the globe, from great inventions to powerful rulers to natural disasters.

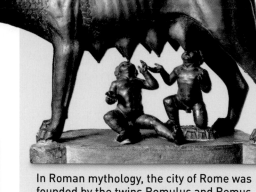

Prehistoric cave paintings are some of the world's oldest pieces of art.

10,000 BCE

- c. 12,000 BCE Cavemen in the Sahara Desert create beautiful cave paintings.
- c. 10,800 BCE Temperatures on Earth start to increase.
- c. 10,000 BCE People start to eat food out of pots and bowls.
- c. 9,000 BCE The earliest stone temples are built in Turkey.
- c. 8,500 BCE A huge stone wall is built around the ancient town of Jericho in the Jordan Valley.
- c. 8,000 BCE Farmers along the Yangtze River in China start to grow rice.

2,000 BCE

- c. 3,600 BCE First wheeled vehicles are invented.
- c. 3,200 BCE Hieroglyphics are written in Ancient Egypt.
- c. 2,590 BCE Great Pyramid is built at Giza, Egypt.
- c. 2,550 BCE Stone circle at Stonehenge is built in England.
- c. 1,700 BCE First plumbing systems are introduced in the Indus Valley (modern-day Pakistan and northwest India).
- c. 1,600 BCE Canaanite people in Western Asia invent the alphabet.

Hieroglyphics used symbols to record messages.

In Roman mythology, the city of Rome was founded by the twins Romulus and Remus. They had been rescued as babies by a wolf.

600 BCE

- c. 753 BCE Founding of the city of Rome.
- c. 650 BCE First coins are minted in Lydia (modern-day Turkey).
- c. 563 BCE Possible birth date of the Buddha in India.
- c. 550 BCE Cyrus the Great of Persia founds the Persian Empire.
- c. 507 BCE Democratic government is introduced in Ancient Greece.
- 448–423 BCE The Parthenon is built in Athens, Greece.

A stone carving of the Buddha

Stone Age
(10,000 BCE)

First farmers
(2,000 BCE)

Iron Age
(600 BCE)

100 CE

- 30 BCE The Ancient Egyptian queen Cleopatra dies.
- 2 CE The world's first recorded census is held in China.
- 79 CE Mount Vesuvius erupts, burying the city of Pompeii in Italy.

Human bodies at Pompeii left shapes in the ash, from which plaster casts have been made.

- c. 100 CE Indian mathematicians invent a number system like the one we use today.
- c. 104 CE Paper is invented by T'sai Lun in China.
- 122–124 CE Hadrian's wall is built in Roman Britain and the Roman Empire is at its greatest extent.

600 CE

- 537 CE Hagia Sophia is completed in Constantinople (modern-day Istanbul, Turkey).
- c. 552 CE Byzantine Emperor Justinian introduces silk production in Europe after smuggling silkworms out of China.
- 600 CE The Maya civilization in Central America is at its height.
- 618 CE The Tang Dynasty is established in China.
- 634–712 CE Muslim Arabs conquer the Middle East, North Africa, and Spain.

Chinese art and culture flourished during the Tang Dynasty.

The astrolabe was used in the Islamic world for navigation.

900 CE

- c. 800 CE Arab navigators perfect the astrolabe, used to predict the positions of the sun, moon, and planets.
- c. 811 CE Paper money is first used in China.
- 868 CE The Diamond Sutra is printed in China. It is the world's oldest surviving printed book.
- c. 872 CE The Vikings discover Iceland.
- c. 900 CE The first castles are built in western Europe.
- 907 CE Collapse of the Tang Dynasty creates disunity in China.

Roman times
(100 CE)

The invaders
(600 CE)

Viking raiders
(900 CE)

The Magna Carta was signed by King John and the English barons.

1200s

- 1180 Angkor Empire of Cambodia reaches its greatest extent.
- 1187 Saladin, Sultan of Egypt and Syria, defeats crusaders and takes Jerusalem.
- 1206 The Mongol Empire is founded by Genghis Khan.
- 1215 The Magna Carta is signed, giving the English people certain rights.
- 1271 The European explorer Marco Polo travels to China.
- c. 1280 Polynesian people discover and settle in New Zealand.

Angkor Wat in Cambodia is the largest temple complex in the world.

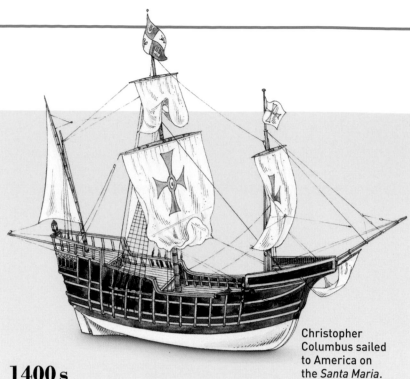

Christopher Columbus sailed to America on the *Santa Maria*.

1400s

- 1405–1433 The Chinese set out on seven major expeditions, traveling as far west as Africa.
- 1421 Beijing becomes the capital of the Ming Empire in China.
- 1453 Ottoman Turks capture Constantinople, ending the Byzantine Empire.
- 1455 The Gutenberg Bible is printed using the first modern printing press.
- 1492 Christopher Columbus lands in America.
- 1492 Christians retake the city of Granada from the Moors, completing the Spanish Reconquest.

Ming tombs were decorated with marble statues like this horse.

Medieval village
(1200s)

Medieval town
(1400s)

1500s

- 1503 Leonardo Da Vinci starts painting the *Mona Lisa*.
- 1509 Henry VIII becomes King of England.
- 1519–33 Spanish conquer the Aztec and Inca empires.
- c. 1530 Beginning of the African slave trade from west Africa to European colonies in the New World.
- 1543 Astronomer Copernicus challenges the view that the Earth is at the center of the Solar System.
- 1596 Englishman John Harrington invents the flush toilet.

The *Mona Lisa* is one of the world's greatest masterpieces.

Galileo spotted the four largest moons around Jupiter.

1600s

- 1609 Italian astronomer Galileo studies the moon, stars, and planets using the newly invented telescope.
- 1618 The English Civil War breaks out.
- 1620 Pilgrims (early settlers) leave England and sail to live in America.
- 1653 The Taj Mahal is completed in Agra, India.
- 1682 The Palace of Versailles is built near Paris, France, for the French king Louis XIV.
- 1687 The scientist Isaac Newton publishes his theory of gravity.

The life of Copernicus is commemorated by this bronze statue.

The Taj Mahal was built by the Mughal emperor Shah Jahan in memory of his wife.

The plague strikes!
(1500s)

Under attack!
(1600s)

1700s

- 1717 The pirate Blackbeard starts plundering ships in the Caribbean.
- 1769 British explorer Captain Cook travels to and maps Australia.
- 1776 U.S. declares independence from Britain.
- 1783 The hot-air balloon is built in France, leading to the first manned flight.
- 1789 The French Revolution begins.
- 1796 English doctor Edward Jenner invents a vaccine against the disease smallpox.

Captain James Cook made three voyages to the Pacific Ocean.

Blackbeard's flag featured a skeleton pointing to a red bleeding heart.

1800s

- 1805 Admiral Lord Nelson defeats the French navy at the Battle of Trafalgar
- 1818 Mary Shelley writes the horror story *Frankenstein*.
- 1819 Simón Bolívar liberates New Granada (now Colombia, Venezuela, and Ecuador) from the Spanish Empire.
- 1826 The world's first photograph is taken.
- 1829 Robert Peel sets up the first police force in London, England.
- 1833 The Slavery Abolition Act is enacted in Britain.

The Slavery Abolition Act was commemorated with coins like this one.

Simón Bolívar became president of the new republic of Granada in South America.

An age of elegance
(1700s)

Grim times
(early 1800s)

Late 1800s

- 1858 Gold is discovered in California, triggering the Gold Rush.
- 1859 Charles Darwin publishes his theory of evolution in *On the Origin of Species*.
- 1865 Slavery is banned in the United States.
- 1872 England plays Scotland in the first international soccer game.
- 1876 Inventor Alexander Graham Bell patents the telephone.
- 1895 Wilhelm Conrad Röntgen takes the first X-ray image.

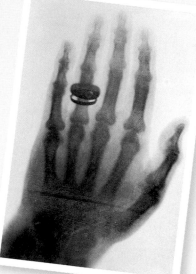

The first X-ray image was of Röntgen's wife's hand.

Other inventors contributed to the invention of the telephone, but Bell was granted the patent.

1900s and 2000s

- 1917 The Russian Revolution leads to the establishment of the first communist state.
- 1939–1945 World War II.
- 1973 First practical cell phone is developed in the United States.
- 1976 Launch of the first Apple computer, which will revolutionize home computing.
- 1989 The Berlin Wall comes down, marking the end of the Cold War.
- 1990 Creation of the World Wide Web leads to the growth of the Internet and e-mail.
- 2011 Completion of the International Space Station.

The Apple I computer was developed by Steve Jobs and Steve Wozniak.

Astronauts live on the International Space Station.

From town to city
(late 1800s)

The street today

GLOSSARY

Amphitheater
An oval or round building with seats. Used by Romans for wild beast shows and gladiator fights.

Amphorae
Clay jars with two handles. Used by Greeks and Romans to store wine and other liquids.

Apothecary
A person who makes and sells medicine.

Atrium
A central courtyard in a Roman house with the rooms opening off it.

Barbarians
Romans referred to people who lived outside the Roman Empire as "barbarians." In particular, the word is often applied to people from north and northeastern Europe who began invading the Empire after 200 CE.

Barrow
An old form of grave, consisting of an earth mound over burial chambers.

Basilica
A Roman building. Law cases and other town functions were held here.

BCE
An abbreviation used in dates. It stands for "Before the Common Era," which covers the period of history before Jesus Christ was believed to have been born.

Booty
Goods or property seized by force.

CE
Stands for the "Common Era," the period after the year Jesus Christ was believed to have been born.

Charter
A written document given by a king or a lord, granting rights to someone.

Cold War
A period of hostility that existed from 1945 to 1989 between the United States and the Soviet Union and its allies. It never resulted in violent warfare.

Coracle
A small oval boat made from woven sticks and covered by a waterproof material.

Crusader
A soldier who engages in a holy war.

Democracy
A government that is elected by the people.

Domus
A Roman town house used by a wealthy family.

Dynasty
A line of rulers of the same family.

Empire
A large area, with different peoples, under the rule of a single powerful state or people.

French Revolution
A period of great social and political upheaval in France, which led to the downfall of the French monarchy and aristocracy.

Gibbet
A wooden gallows where dangerous criminals were put to death by hanging.

Guildhall
A place where guild members (see guilds) met to run their guilds and the town.

Guilds
Unions of craftsmen or merchants that controlled working standards, conditions, and prices. They also cared for members in trouble.

Hieroglyphics
An Ancient Egyptian writing system using picture symbols carved in stone.

Harpoon
A spearlike weapon used to kill or capture prey.

Industrial Revolution
A period during the 1700s and 1800s when there were huge changes in the way people lived and worked. This was brought about by new inventions that led to factories producing goods faster than people could at home.

Iron Age
Although people were experimenting with iron by 1,100 BCE, the period of history known as the Iron Age began around 900 BCE, when iron replaced bronze for making tools and weapons.

Jetty
A landing place on a river or in a harbor.

Keep
A stone building that was the inner stronghold of the castle.

Longship
A Viking warship with oars and a square sail.

Nomads
People who wander from place to place seeking food and shelter.

Palisade
A fence of strong wooden poles built around a fort or village to help defend it from enemies and wild animals.

Patent
A document granting an inventor sole rights to an invention.

Peddler
A travelling salesman.

Plow
A machine or tool used in farming to prepare the soil for sowing seeds.

Recycling
A process that turns used materials into new products.

Roman Empire
Around 200 BCE, Rome began conquering other lands and created an empire that was to last in Western Europe until 476 CE. At its height, it covered much of Europe, North Africa, and parts of the Middle East.

Sickle
A handheld tool usually with a curved blade used to cut crops.

Sling
A piece of leather or woven material used to hurl stones.

Spanish Reconquest
A period of almost 800 years during the Middle Ages when Christian kingdoms succeeded in retaking areas of Muslim-controlled Spain.

Stocks
A wooden frame with holes for feet, neck, and hands. It was used to punish small-time criminals.

Stone Age
A period of history lasting approximately 2.5 million years when tools and weapons were made mostly of stone. It began when the earliest people made their first tools and lasted until metal was introduced.

Suburb
An area on the outskirts of a city where people live.

Sulfur
A yellow mineral that burns with a choking smoke and horrible smell.

Thatched roof
A roof made of straw.

Threshing
Beating a harvested cereal plant to separate the seeds.

Vaccine
An injection that increases the body's immunity from a disease.

Vikings
Fierce warriors from Norway, Sweden, and Denmark. They raided and settled in parts of Europe between 790 and 1100 CE.

Winnowing
Tossing grains into the air to separate them from their light cases.

INDEX

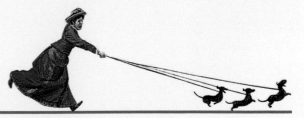

CREDITS

DK would like to thank:
Jenny Sich for proofreading, Jackie Brind for the index, John Searcy for Americanization, and Philip Parker for historical consultancy.

The Publisher would like to thank the following for their kind permission to reproduce

their photographs:

a=above, c=center, b=below, l=left, r=right, t=top

38 Dorling Kindersley: Ashmolean Museum, Oxford (crb). **Getty Images:** De Agostini (tr); Danita Delimont (tl). **39 Dorling Kindersley:** Museo Archeologico Nazionale di Napoli (cl); National Maritime Museum, London (tr). **40 Corbis:** (tl). **Dorling Kindersley:** Bethany Dawn (cl). **41 Corbis:** Bettmann (tr). **Dorling**

Kindersley: Musee du Louvre, Paris (tl). **42 Getty Images:** (tr). **43 Corbis:** Bettmann (ca). **Dorling Kindersley:** Science Museum, London (clb). **NASA:** (crb). **SuperStock:** Science and Society (tr)

All other images © Dorling Kindersley
For further information see: www.dkimages.com